NOW GO

SELL

SOMEBODY SOMETHING!

Steve –
GROW GET 'em!
Bryan Flanagan

INSPIRATION FOR SALESPEOPLE

NOW GO

SELL

SOMEBODY SOMETHING!

BRYAN FLANAGAN

Now Go Sell Somebody Something: Inspiration for Salespeople
© 2005 Bryan Flanagan

Manufactured in the United States of America.

For information, please contact:
Brown Books Publishing Group
16200 North Dallas Parkway, Suite 170
Dallas, Texas 75248
www.brownbooks.com
972-381-0009

ISBN 0-9753907-7-5
LCCN 2005920122
2 3 4 5 6 7 8 9 10

A BOOK THAT EVEN A MOTHER-IN-LAW LOVES:

I've known Bryan for over thirty-five years, and he has always been an encourager to others. In this book, he is a salesperson's top cheerleader.

—Margery Kadi, Bryan's mother-in-law

I am no salesman; I fear rejection too much. After reading this book, however, I began to feel "I could sell that." Further, should I not make the sale I am not a failure. In an engaging and conversational style, Bryan Flanagan has written a much needed book, one that addresses the psyche of the salesperson.

—Harry Chase, Retired minister, Bryan's Sunday school teacher

Whether you are a rookie or a veteran of the sales game, you'll benefit from this book. Why? Because Bryan reminds you to have fun and to enjoy your selling efforts.

—Jeff Fletcher, twenty-one-year sales veteran

You'll enjoy Bryan's philosophy of selling and you'll gain from his real world sales stories. After each chapter, you'll want to go sell somebody something!

—Charlie Jenkins, thirty-year-sales veteran

DEDICATION

The Wind Beneath My Wingtips

Maybe you've heard of this old saying: if you see a turtle on top of a fence post, you know he had help getting up there. This certainly pertains to the world of selling. As sales professionals, we don't succeed in a vacuum; our success is part of a team effort. We all need others who will support us, encourage us, and cheer us on. I've been blessed to have one such person in my life.

The degree of success I have experienced as a sales professional is in large part due to the assistance, support, and encouragement of my wife,

Cyndi. Although I have given up on myself quite a few times, she has never given up on me. This book would not be in your hands had it not been for her.

As for my background, I invested fourteen years with the IBM Corporation as a salesman, as a people manager, and as a sales instructor at the National Training Center. I may date myself here, but I sold electronic typewriters and copying machines for IBM's old Office Products Division. Yes, for the younger readers, at one time IBM manufactured and sold the finest typewriters in the world! That was back in the days when IBM'ers wore dark suits, white shirts, and fourteen-pound wingtip shoes!

I began at IBM as a delivery boy during my "second senior year" at Louisiana State University in Baton Rouge, Louisiana. Cyndi and I were married that year, and upon graduation I was hired full time as an IBM salesman. When I finished my training, I was given a rookie territory consisting of six parishes (Louisiana for "counties") down the Mississippi River. But there was a problem. You see, I couldn't sell. I was a very ineffective salesman. In fact, I was ineffective for the entire six years I sold in the Baton Rouge office. I was in sales, but sales was not in me. While I struggled those first years,

Cyndi was achieving great success as a first-grade schoolteacher. She loved those kids, and she even loved their parents. She really enjoyed her profession. She experienced victory after victory while I had limited success, at best. Yet she cheered me on countless times. She was always there to boost my spirits and encourage me. I tried to quit on myself several times, but she would not allow me to quit.

One of the biggest events in my professional career occurred during my sixth year with IBM. My goal was to be promoted to national sales instructor. But my sales performance never qualified me to be in the top 10 percent of the sales force, so I thought this promotion was an impossibility. However, I received an invitation in June 1977 to be a guest instructor at the National Training Center in Dallas, Texas.

The guest instructor role required the field sales representative (me) to audition for two weeks during basic training for new Office Product Division salespeople. The responsibilities included working with the new hires in the areas of selling skills, product knowledge, demonstration skills and sales interviews. This audition also required a ninety-minute-long formal presentation on a topic relating to a specific selling skill.

If the guest instructor was effective, he or she would be invited to join an elite staff of twenty full-time staff instructors. This two- to three-year assignment positioned one to return to the field as a sales manager. I couldn't sell very well, but I thought I could teach others! Those who can, do. Those who can't, teach. And those who can't teach, teach selling!

The promotion usually rested on how well the guest instructor presented his or her ninety-minute sales training program. I put so much pressure on myself that I was having trouble completing my assignment: I was about to forfeit my only chance for the position of sales instructor. On the Thursday before I was to leave for Dallas, I remember sitting on the couch in our family room giving myself a pity party. I was upset; I was crying; I was really down on myself.

Cyndi heard all of the moaning, groaning, and carrying on that I could dish out. Finally, she'd heard enough and she'd had enough. With love and sensitivity toward her hurting husband, she really let me have it.

"Bryan, you're ready for this. Everything you've done in the past six years has prepared you for this. Every Wednesday night for the past five years you've poured your heart into Toastmasters, getting ready for this next two weeks. You've volunteered to train every new salesperson in the branch for the past five years. Each one has been successful because of your training. You have a teacher's heart, and you know how hard it is for new salespeople to be successful. You're prepared for the next two weeks. I believe you are ready. Your boss believes you are ready, or he wouldn't have approved that you go. We all believe it. But you've got to believe it!"

Then, in a more gentle way, she encouraged me to talk it out with her so that I could see the real reason for the fear behind my feelings. She knew that I was afraid of failing at my one chance for this promotion. She then assured me that she would love me whether I was a salesman, a sales instructor, or a high school basketball coach. What happened during the next two weeks was not going to change her devotion and love for me. WOW!

With that encouragement and love, I went to Dallas and for two weeks had the time of my life. Cyndi gave me the inspiration to overcome my fears so that I could move into the sales instructor's role. Shortly after the training session, I was promoted to the national sales training position.

This is just one of countless examples of how Cyndi has been "the wind beneath my wingtips." I am so blessed that she is a part of my life.

Since 1970, Cyndi and I have learned to see through each other—and we still enjoy the view!

Cyndi, thank you for sharing your life and your love with me.

Bryan Flanagan
Dallas, Texas, January 2005

CONTENTS

ACKNOWLEDGMENTS

As a sports enthusiast, I have often heard the term "home field advantage." It seems that the home team has an advantage in winning games when played in their home stadium. The home team is surrounded by fans who support, cheer, and encourage the players. That's a substantial advantage.

Throughout my entire sales career, I have enjoyed the home field advantage. I would like to thank my "teammates" for all the support and encouragement they have given me.

My Home Team:

My mother and father were not only great parents, they were also great people. They always encouraged me to make the most of my God-given talents. Dad, thank you for instilling in each of your children a solid work ethic. Mama, I continually gain encouragement from your strength and determination. Brother Pat, I don't know if you remember the valuable lesson you taught me about self-belief. Early in my sales career, you heard me say that I could never imagine earning $100,000 a year as a salesperson; you straightened me out. You said, "Until you imagine it, you'll never earn it." What a great lesson. Kathy, thank you for always believing in and encouraging your little brother. Whether it was supporting me to run for student council president or urging me to join a fraternity at LSU, you were always in my corner.

My Fraternity Team:

The bonds of my fraternity last forever. I learned so much from each of my fraternity brothers. I absorbed friendship, justice, and learning during those days as an active member. Thanks for living the Spirit of Sigma Chi.

My IBM Team:

Fred Kelpe believed in me when I didn't believe in myself. Fred, thanks for transforming this delivery boy into a sales professional. Dick Geoffroy, thanks for encouraging me to pursue my dreams as a sales instructor. Dan McCarty, thanks for dragging me to my first Toastmasters Club meeting: that was the boost to my confidence that I really needed. Phil Callahan, thanks for modeling the difference between a sales manager and a "people manager." I continue to use the lessons you taught me.

My Zig Ziglar Team:
Zig Ziglar is the most consistent man I have ever met. I am proud to work for him and to call him my friend. Zig, thanks for touching so many lives and thanks for touching my heart. To all my co-workers over the years, thank you for allowing me to be part of your team.

My Customer Team:
Thank you for trusting me enough to invest time, energy, and finances in my training programs. I continually say this while training your people: "I learn more than you do!"

My Friendship Team:
Ralph Walts, I miss you every day. There was never a better best friend than you. Thanks for challenging me to dream big. Eddie Samson, thanks for making so many journeys with me. Your shoulder was always available. Bill Siegrist, thank you for

guiding me through all those spiritual questions. I see Christ through you.

My Publishing Team:
Milli Brown, thanks for your patience with me. We can tease about it now, but you and your entire team at Brown Books know exactly how long this project took. Kathryn and Erica, thanks for holding my hand through this process.

My Sales Team:
Thanks to all those salespeople who work hard each and every day to elevate this vocation to a professional level. I admire each of you. Let's never forget that our profession is an honorable one.

My Family Team:
Cyndi, thanks for loving me when I was not lovable. You are a constant source of inspiration and strength. Thanks for being my wife. Thanks for loving and guiding our children. You are simply the best! Patrick, thank you for who you are and what you are becoming. I am so proud to be your dad. Quinn, thank you for your courage and determination. You are certainly the "lemonade maker" in our family. Your daddy loves his little girl.

FOREWORD

For the past fifty-eight years I have been a salesman. I know that in the world of sales there are many challenges and a great deal of stress. How you handle those challenges and that stress will ultimately determine your sales success. In this book, you'll get that check-up from the neck up to build yourself and your sales career. You'll get the encouragement you need to keep going in those uncertain times.

In my book *Secrets of Closing the Sale* I state that your attitude makes the difference in sales. The information Bryan shares in his book will help build your attitude toward sales and the sales profession.

Bryan Flanagan has been a trusted friend and coworker for the past twenty-plus years. I have come to respect his passion for the sales profession and his willingness to help others succeed in the world of sales. He reminds us that we don't have to like everything about sales to be successful. He will challenge you to increase your skills, your knowledge, and your attitude toward selling. He will inspire you to honor your profession. He'll impel you to recapture your passion for what you do. And he'll stimulate you to enjoy what you do.

As you read you will come to know that Bryan Flanagan has his head knowledge and experience in high gear. By the time you finish *Now, Go Sell Somebody Something!* you will know that his heart for the sales profession is the driving force in his career. That combination will enable you to go sell somebody something right now! Which means I'll see you *Over the Top* in the world of selling!

Zig Ziglar

PREFACE

In the sales workshops I conduct for Ziglar Training Systems, I ask the audience, "What do you like about the sales profession, and what do you dislike about the sales profession?" The answers are listed on a flip chart in the front of the room.

These are the answers I often receive:

What I LIKE:	What I DISLIKE:
Freedom	Rejection
People	Uncertainty
Solving problems	The ups and downs
Money	The pressure
Controlling my future	Monthly quota

I then ask, "What is the common denominator between these two lists?" As you will notice, there is not one policy, procedure, or product listed. Therefore, what is the connection between the two?

Here it comes. Are you ready? The connection is how the salesperson handles the emotional demands of the sales profession. Selling is one of the most stressful professions out there.

Let's compare the accounting profession to that of sales. I admire accountants because I can't do what they do. (Do you know what happens when my bankbook doesn't balance? I change banks!) I don't have an analytical bone in my body, but maybe you do: How long is the interval between reporting periods for an accountant? One month? One quarter? One year? What is the reporting period for a salesperson? Every door knock, every phone call, and every handshake. Our reporting periods come fast and furious! We are going to hear "no" more often than accountants do. We have more opportunities to fail than accountants. Therefore, we must be emotionally stronger than they are! One of the reasons I love selling is because success doesn't depend on the color of your skin. It does depend on the thickness of your skin.

Let me share a story with you. I was once going through a tough time as a salesman. As regional director of a new company in Dallas, I was prospecting almost full time and was having a very difficult time with it. Of course, for several weeks, I brought all that frustration home with me. Cyndi suggested that I set an appointment with her friend Mary, who was a counselor. I protested because I didn't think Mary could offer any assistance in my situation. Besides, she charged $100 per hour for her counseling services! Well, I'm about to save you at least a hundred bucks because the advice I received was worth a lot more than what she charged.

After we'd talked for a few minutes, Mary said, "Bryan, why don't you admit that you don't like to sell anymore?"

I said, "But I do like to sell. I've worked very hard to be an effective salesperson, and to admit that I don't like selling wouldn't be the truth."

So we talked a few more minutes, and Mary said, "Okay. Then admit there is an aspect of selling that you don't like."

I said, "Well, I can certainly do that. I hate prospecting. I hate everything about it. It is humbling, depressing, and frustrating!"

What Mary said next was some of the finest sales education I've ever received. She smiled and said, "That's okay."

WOW! "That's okay," equates to $50 a word, but man, was it worth it! What she was saying to me was my wake-up call. She was in fact telling me, "That's okay: you don't have to like everything about selling to be outrageously successful at it."

And this revelation didn't apply only to selling, but to any undertaking in life. My wife and I have two of the greatest kids anyone could have. Patrick and Quinn have given us joy and happiness beyond our wildest dreams. I love those two as much as a man can love his children. However, there are some things about "daddyhood" that I don't like. There are some very painful events in the life of a father. But they don't stop me from being successful as a dad.

Mary's comment was so liberating for me. You see, what she was saying was this: "You don't have to like it; you just have to do it!" As soon as she told me that, I immediately became a better prospector. Why? Because I was liberated. Because I took my foot off my throat and gave myself permission to be successful. I realized I didn't have to like prospecting to be good at it: I could be effective, even though I didn't enjoy it.

The same is true for you. You don't have to like everything about selling to be outrageously successful at it. You just have to do it.

The purpose of this book is to encourage you to be successful as a sales professional. It is not a book on how to open and close sales. This book is intended to give courage to your selling efforts, to increase your confidence, and to inspire you to greater sales victories. This book is an attempt to encourage you and, in some cases, to entertain you.

It is my sincere desire that you will pick up this book and read it when you need a "checkup from the neck up," or a motivational lift, before you make the next sales call. It is my sincere desire that the messages in this book will help you deal more effectively with the emotional demands of the selling profession. Good luck and good selling.

Now, go sell somebody something!

YOUR CLOSING ATTITUDE IS MORE IMPORTANT THAN YOUR CLOSING SKILL

Several weeks ago, I was speaking with Jay Hellwig, a top sales professional. Jay said, "Zig Ziglar's CD program on closing the sale is my all-time favorite. Since I've been listening to those CDs, I've closed more sales."

That program has more than fifty specific closing techniques. I asked Jay what he considered his favorite.

Jay thought for a moment and said, "Oh, I don't have a favorite closing technique."

I asked, "You just said that they helped you close sales. But if you aren't using the techniques, how can it be your favorite program?"

Jay taught me a valuable lesson with his answer. He said, "That's easy. The program didn't give me a closing technique. It gave me a closing attitude!"

A closing attitude. Now that is powerful.

Jay is right. The way you feel about closing the order is often more important than the technique you use to close the sale. You probably have a number of strong closes. However, if you lack a strong closing attitude, you may never use those closes.

Have you thought about your closing attitude lately? What is your attitude about closing the sale? Remember, closing is what you do with the prospect, not something you do to the prospect. Closing should be the logical conclusion to your selling activities. It should not be the stage of the sales process that is adversarial between the seller and the buyer. The buyer should be as eager for this stage of the process as the seller is.

Why do you ask people to buy from you? You ask people to buy from you so that you can feed your family, not your ego. If you don't want to bruise your ego, you may be hesitant to ask for the order. However, if you hesitate enough times, you are not putting bread on your family's table.

What happens when you ask for the order and you get it? You win! But what happens when you ask for the order and you don't get it? Well, you don't lose—you break even. That's right, you break even. You can't lose by doing your job. Your job is to ask people to exchange money for your products and services. When you perform your job in a professional manner, you have every right to ask the prospect to buy from you.

When you ask the prospect to purchase from you today, he or she wants to know that you believe his or her decision is a correct one. You can assist with this if you have a positive closing attitude. You need to exhibit confidence during this stage of the process. If you do, you will be able to expect sales success, not hope for sales success.

Jay Hellwig is right. Your closing attitude is more important than your closing technique!

Now, go sell somebody something!

Sales Slumps: Don't You Hate 'Em? Here's a Couple of Things to Do About 'Em!

All Major League baseball players experience batting slumps during the season. Former big-league catcher Terry Kennedy said, "Most slumps are like the common cold. They last two weeks, no matter what you do!"

Sales professionals have something in common with professional ballplayers. That is, all high-achieving, high-performing sales professionals have either just climbed out of a sales slump, they are in a sales slump now, or (guess what) they are about to get into a sales slump! It's gonna happen!

Your objective is to try to eliminate as many as you can and shorten the duration for those you cannot eliminate. Let's take a look at six methods to shorten the length of these sales slumps. (If you allow a slump to last too long, you will walk around your office looking like the picture on your driver's license! That's not a pretty sight.)

1. **Return to the Basics.** What activities were you doing when things were going well that you aren't doing now? Were you using the same prospecting techniques, the same questioning methodology, similar presentation strategies? If you began repeating those positive activities and behaviors, would you realize better results? Sales basics are what brought you this far; don't abandon them now.

2. **Keep a Mental Victory List.** Remind yourself of your past sales success and victories. This mental victory list should include all those things that gave you the most satisfaction and confidence as a sales professional. This may include the time you won the account in a very tough, competitive battle. You may want to remind yourself of how you "saved" an account. Think in terms of your persistence, your selling skills, and your sensitivity to meeting the needs of prospects.

3. **Visit a Satisfied Client.** This is a great way to give yourself a "checkup from the neck up." Choose a few clients who have had successful relationships with you and your company, and visit them! If that's not feasible, call or e-mail them. Contact them so that you will be reminded of all the good service you have provided for them. This will give you a renewed energy for what you do and for the products and services you provide.

4. **Enroll in "Automobile University."** In other words, feed the upper end of your body. When you get hungry, you feed the lower portion of your body; when you are in a slump, you should feed the upper portion of your body. You need to put the pure, the powerful, the clean and the positive in your mind. This can be accomplished by listening to a motivational tape or CD while you are driving. Instead of listening to talk radio, plug in a tape or CD before you get into the slump. Don't wait until you are in the middle of the slump. Be assertive by taking action. We all need to replace our negative self-talk with a positive mind-set. Automobile University allows you to achieve this mind-set.

5. **Develop Selective Memory.** You should not "major on minors." In other words, don't focus

on past problems. Remember the good things you've done and are capable of doing. You must learn to focus on your major strengths. Use the FIDO principle. This means Forget It and Drive On. Don't dwell on past mistakes, errors or lost sales. Focus your full attention on your good traits and qualities. Shake off the dust and move to the next challenge.

6. **Don't Compare Your Abilities to Your Experiences.** You have very limited control over prospects' missing meetings or canceling appointments. You have no control over the national economy. You do have control over how you handle your response to those things. If your present set of circumstances is not good, that does not mean your present skill set is not good. You still have good abilities and skills. It's just that the circumstances aren't good. You gotta believe in yourself. Keep the faith!

Sales slumps are going to happen. You must shorten their duration and work your way out of these slumps. If you follow the above methods, you'll improve your sales effectiveness and consistency.

Now, go sell somebody something!

SALESPEOPLE, MAKE A COMMITMENT

I recently saw an old black-and-white Western movie. The bad guys outnumbered the good gunslinger (I think it was Gregory Peck). He had a buddy who was present but could not make up his mind whose side to join. Peck told him, "Billy, make a commitment. Until you commit, Billy, you're just taking up space!"

Commitment. It can be the difference between winning and losing. Or it can be the one element that determines your sales success!

Football coach Lou Holtz addresses commitment through the following story. At practice one day, he noticed the left guard was just going through the motions, not really giving it his best effort. Coach Holtz removed him from the offensive line during a scrimmage and told him to sit on the sidelines. He then began running the plays without his left guard. The offensive team only had ten players against the defensive team's eleven players. Coach Holtz instructed the running back to run the football to the area where the left guard normally played. Because there was no one to block for the running back, he was tackled each time.

After this happened several times, the offensive players came back to the huddle grumbling and complaining. When Coach Holtz asked why, they told him they would get beat if they did not have a left guard to block. Holtz taught the entire team a great lesson when he replied, "I would rather walk into a football stadium with ten committed players and lose a game than I would with someone on the team who is not committed."

Now, the left guard had looked like a football player that day in practice. He put his uniform on like a football player. He talked like a football player. He even ran like a football player. Yet he'd never made a commitment to be a football player.

There are salespeople just like this football player. They look like salespeople. They put on their "uniforms" like salespeople. They even talk like salespeople. Yet they never perform like salespeople because they have never made a commitment to be a sales professional.

All salespeople need to commit to the sales profession. When we do commit, our families benefit, our companies benefit, and our clients benefit. Take a few moments each day to commit to your profession, to your teammates and to yourself.

Until you commit, you are just like Billy. You are just taking up space.

Now, go sell somebody something!

THE LIGHTER SIDE OF SELLING

S elling is a difficult way to make a living. Just think about it: if selling were easy, your manager would still be doing it!

Successful salespeople have learned to cope with the emotional demands of their profession by using a technique that has served them well over the years. Other professions also use this technique, but it seems that salespeople have perfected this technique because we need it and use it more than others. This technique is called a "sense of humor." Because we salespeople run into more resistance and rejection than most other professionals, we need a heightened sense of humor. The main benefits of maintaining a sense of humor are that we enjoy the profession more; we interact with others more effectively; humor relaxes the client-salesperson relationship; and it puts more pep in our step! Humor is also a biblical principle. In Proverbs 14:30 we learn that "A relaxed attitude lengthens a man's life." I hope the following stories put a smile on your face and lengthen your life.

A salesman and his wife arrive home one evening to find a burglar in their house. The burglar says, "You saw my face; now I have to shoot you. But I always know my victims' names. What's your name?" The wife says, "My name is Alice." The burglar says, "I can't shoot you. That's my mother's name." He then turns to the salesman and asks, "What's your name?" And the quick-thinking salesman says, "My name is Ralph. But my friends call me Alice!"

A farmer complains to the veterinarian, "I'm trying to sell my mule, but sometimes he limps and sometimes he doesn't." The vet replies, "Sell him when he's not limping!"

One saleslady to another: "I don't want to take my troubles to bed with me, but my husband won't sleep alone."

One salesman to another: "My business is so bad that even my customers who don't intend to pay aren't buying."

The sales rep went to the sales manager and says, "I want a raise." The manager replies, "You don't get a raise until you've been here five years." The salesman says, "But I've been here seven years!" The manager says, "Sorry, but you should have asked two years ago!"

Invest in laughter. It will improve your face value!

Now, go sell somebody something!

Sales Managers: Increase Your Sales Meeting Effectiveness

When was the last time a sales meeting actually addressed sales? It seems that most sales meetings focus on everything except selling and sales skills enhancement. These days, the subjects discussed at sales meetings are in the areas of administrative and procedural issues or policy changes. Rarely do these meetings address sales skills, selling techniques, or sales training.

With that in mind, here are some ideas that you can use at an upcoming sales meeting. These focus on training issues and are designed to increase sales effectiveness. If you are not a sales manager, perhaps you can volunteer to conduct the next sales meeting.

Or you can suggest that your manager address some of these topics at the next sales meeting.

1. **Sales Objections Clinic:** With input from your sales team, create a list of common objections you receive from prospects or customers. If possible, categorize this list into topics: financial (budget, price), features, functions, competitive concerns, or contractual issues (terms and conditions). Assign one category to a team of reps and instruct them to discuss effective answers for their assigned objection. Each group then reports to the entire team on specific ways to answer those objections. Ask each team to submit written answers so that you can distribute these to each salesperson at the conclusion of the meeting.

2. **Referral Practice:** Prior to the meeting, assign each salesperson the task of creating five ways to ask for referrals. Each person will then share those ideas with the rest of the team. You may want to give an award for the sales rep with the most creative method of securing referrals.

3. **Sales Call Role-Playing:** Here's a training method that most reps tend to avoid: the dreaded "role-play" exercise. This practice is very effective, yet at the same time it produces the most anxiety. Why? Because we feel pres-

sure when performing in front of our peers—
and our boss. However, if the manager sets the
stage correctly, you can achieve great returns
from role-plays. Here are some guidelines:

- Emphasize that the purpose is to practice for
  technique, not results. When I work with our
  clients, I point out that "You want to learn in
  class so you are not penalized in cash!"

- Make the role-play real, giving it as much
  real-world flavor as possible. Instruct both
  the "customer" and the "rep" to stay in role
  for the duration of the role-play.

- Create the role-play so that there is a minimum
  of surprises. Give specific instructions so that
  both parties clearly understand their roles.

- Give feedback based on specific, observ-
  able behavior. Emphasis should be placed
  on what was done well and the areas that
  need to be improved. This requires the manager to take detailed notes and provide specific examples in order to add value to the
  debriefing session.

- Create a learning atmosphere by giving specific objectives for each role-play exercise.
  Clearly explain those objectives. If the pur-

pose is to practice questioning skills, sell benefits or close the sale, you should clearly communicate that to the participants.

Obviously, you will have to modify these topics to best fit your environment; however, that is well worth the effort. Once you do so, your sales meetings will actually address selling and selling skills!

Now, go sell somebody something!

PROCRASTINATION: READ THIS NOW!

(Or you can wait till later.)

(No, read it now!)

To procrastinate is to defer to take action, to put off doing something until later. It is derived from Latin, literally meaning "move tomorrow forward." I am the master of procrastination. I say this because I was supposed to write this book last year. Oh, well . . .

Procrastination comes in various shapes, forms, and sizes. It affects all people in all walks of life. For the student, procrastination means pulling an all-nighter. For the busy parent, it means spending time with the kids when there is a lull in the week, month, or year. For the spouse, it's scheduling that much-needed vacation when there is a convenient time of year. For the salesperson, it's making that difficult sales call "when I get around to it." We are all guilty of this. Then we complicate the problem because we are also perfectionists! That's a dangerous combination: a perfectionist, who procrastinates. That describes a surefire ulcer candidate. (It's not what you eat that causes ulcers—it's what's eating you!)

How do people control and conquer procrastination? Let's attack it from three angles:

1. Why do we procrastinate?

2. What tasks do we put off starting or completing?

3. How do we overcome procrastination?

Why do we procrastinate? You may have your own specific reasons, but generally we procrastinate for some or all of the following:

- It is an unpleasant task.

- The size of the task overwhelms us.

- We've not set this activity/task as a priority.

- We tend to "major on minors" by failing to prioritize.

- We try to avoid negative situations.

- We develop paralysis of analysis.

- We lack confidence and fear that we may fail at this endeavor.

As you can see, there are many reasons why we procrastinate.

What tasks do we put off completing? Each individual has his or her own answers to this one. It depends on your career, the tasks required of you, and the skill and attitude you bring to each task. However, we can all agree that we tend to avoid those things that are most difficult for us or those areas in which we have the least willpower. It may be losing weight, starting an exercise program, quitting the smoking habit, writing that difficult proposal, making cold calls, or getting enough sleep each night. It is important to identify those tasks that we tend to avoid completing. That is a great start.

How do we overcome procrastination? I will tell you in a later chapter. No, just kidding. There are five steps in achieving this, as follows:

1. Make a commitment to solve the problem. How serious are you about this? Will you do what is necessary to overcome procrastination? If so, continue reading. If not, you need to learn to live with putting things off.

2. Prioritize your tasks each day. Rank those tasks in order of importance. Commit to accomplish the most difficult ones first.

3. For the larger tasks, use the "divide and conquer" technique. That is, break the tasks into smaller pieces and accomplish each major task in smaller, more manageable segments. Also, look for the opportunity to delegate parts of the task to others.

4. Establish timelines and deadlines. We all work better when we have an understanding of pending deadlines. Give yourself deadlines to achieve. For larger projects, we are motivated when we achieve smaller victories that lead to the overall victory. You can include incentives or rewards for yourself as you meet each deadline.

5. Enjoy the journey. Let's face it, this task must be done, and you must do it. You might as well enjoy the process of completing it. You can discipline yourself to achieve great things and still have fun along the way.

Well, there you have it. Procrastination can be conquered. Usually, we have to conquer ourselves first, but it can be done! Best of luck. And, hey, why don't you begin to prioritize your list right now!

Now, go sell somebody something!

K.I.S.S.

(Yeah, it's old, but it still applies to you!)

Baseball Hall of Famer Willie Mays described the game of baseball: "They throw it, I hit it. They hit it, I catch it." Simple and straightforward.

Arnold Palmer's father gave his son this advice: "Hit the ball hard. Go find it. Hit it hard again." Simple and straightforward.

Why can't selling be that simple and straight-forward? Well, selling can be and should be that simple. In its simplest form, selling is nothing more than a communication process. You talk to the prospect and determine her needs, situations, challenges, and problems. You then communicate the value of your solution. Simple and straightforward. The process need not be complicated.

Today, tell the prospect you want to know more about him, his business, the goals he has in place, and the barriers to those goals. Then interpret the value and advantages that you have to offer to your prospect. Simple and straightforward.

Keep it simple, salesperson!

Now, go sell somebody something!

Prose for the Pros: Part I—Boss, I Got Better Things to Do!

When the sales manager asked the rep, "What are you up to?"

The sales rep replied, "Boss, I got lots and lots to do."

When the sales manager asked, "Shouldn't you be out making calls?"

The sales rep stared blankly at the office walls.

"Making calls is important, but I got better things to do.

Like letters and proposals, I got a whole slew.

I've got phone calls to return and paperwork to churn.

Business cards to file and I need to work on my smile.

You gave me a prime territory and I'll go through it

Once I clean my desk, I will certainly get to it.

Oh, I'll make my sales calls. In fact I'll make a whole bunch.

But I'm reserving all my strength for today's power lunch.

How many calls, Boss? So many it's hard to tell.

But right after lunch, I'm gonna go out there and sell.

There's no hesitancy in me, no sir, not one iota.

Just wait till tomorrow, and I'll show you how to make quota."

Now, go sell somebody something!

Look Behind the Milk!

Cyndi and I recently celebrated our thirty-fourth wedding anniversary—it's been the best twenty-nine years of her life! After all these years, Cyndi knows me very well. She knows that I can't find a thing in our house. She may not know where some items are either, but she looks until she locates them. I take the easy way out by asking her to find them for me. But she's smarter than that. For example, when I open the refrigerator, she knows that I am going to ask her, "Where are the pickles?" or "Where'd you put the grape jelly?" I know these things are somewhere in there. Each time I ask, she has an automatic response: "Bryan, it's not going to find you. Just look behind the milk!" And each time I move the milk and look behind it, I find the item I'm searching for. I just hate it when that happens!

Isn't this a lot like prospecting for new customers? Our future customers are out there—we just have to "look behind the milk." We can't wait for the prospects to find us! Oh, we can make a sale when the customers find us, but that doesn't happen enough to make a livelihood! Therefore, we must move the milk, or pick up the phone, or knock on a few doors, or join a networking group in order to find our prospects.

How are you identifying your future customers? Are you making a set number of prospecting calls each day? Are you telling your barber, the owner of your dry cleaner, or your fellow Little League parents to recommend you to their contacts? Have you asked your current clients for referrals?

Your customers aren't always going to find you. You may have to "move the milk" in order to find them.

Now, go sell somebody something!

RESOLUTIONS FOR THE SALES PROFESSIONAL

I t doesn't have to be a new year for you to implement these sales resolutions.

I, as a professional salesperson, resolve to:

1. Listen so that my clients will talk, and talk so that my clients will listen. I will improve my listening skills by focusing on the other person. I must remember that when I get wrapped up in myself, I have a small package.

2. Maintain a professional appearance. I will look the part of a successful sales professional. I will dress appropriately for my client base. If I wear a three-piece suit, I will make sure at least two

pieces match!

3. Floss at least once a day.

4. Continue to learn my profession. Since you never graduate from selling, I will invest in sales training material, I will attend at least two sales training courses, and I will enroll in "Automobile University." I will become more dangerous than I am right now!

5. Better prepare for each and every sales day. This way, I can eliminate many daily surprises. My preparation compensates for any deficits in talent!

6. Separate refusal from rejection. One is professional, the other personal. My clients don't know me well enough to personally reject me. Therefore, I will accept a client's saying "no" as a refusal to buy from me, the professional. I will not take it personally. A "no" today moves me closer to a "yes" tomorrow.

7. Never miss an opportunity to laugh at myself. I will take the clients and their needs seriously; I will take myself less seriously. (Angels fly because they take themselves lightly!) I will laugh at myself at least once a day!

8. Enjoy the sales profession more this year than any year in the past! I am in the helping profession. I help my clients save money, help them improve their lifestyle, and help solve their problems. I help my clients win! I will continue to be proud of my profession.

Now, go sell somebody something!

Succeed with E's

oes sales success require hard work? Determination? Dedication? Perserverance? Yes, of
course, it does. However, you can also E's into success. Here are three ways to do so:

Energy: We need energy to start and complete
tasks. Oftentimes the energy is propelled by the
passion we have for the task at hand. The energy
turns into enthusiasm. Others can see this energy.
It is shown in our smiles, in our attitude, and in
the pride in our stride. Others get excited by your
energy! Set yourself on fire with enthusiasm, and
people will come from miles to watch you burn!

Ego-Drive: Ego-drive asks, "How much are you willing to give for success?" How willing are you to do the difficult things in order to reap the rewards of success? Victor Hugo wrote, "People don't lack courage, they lack will." Ego-drive triggers your will to succeed. Ego-drive translates into confidence—not conceit. (Conceit is a weird disease that makes everyone sick except the person who has it.) Ego-drive also translates into determination. Some people succeed because they are destined to succeed, but most people succeed because they are determined to succeed.

Empathy: We are all in the people business; therefore, we must be tuned into people, not tuned into policies, procedures, practices, or products. Every person you encounter today is tuned into radio station WII-FM. This stands for "What's In It For Me?" By tuning into the other person's radio station you create connection; by broadcasting your own radio station, you create static! When you tune into the other person's radio station you can sincerely care for him; you can empathize with him. We are not on this earth to see through people; we are on this earth to see people through.

The challenge today is to E's into success by using your Energy, your Ego-drive, and your Empathy.

You do not pay the price for success—you enjoy the benefits of success.

Now, go sell somebody something!

There Is No "I" in "Team" . . . But There Is in "Win"!

When Phil Jackson became the coach of the NBA's Chicago Bulls, he called a team meeting after practice. He told his players, "There is no 'I' in 'team'!" Michael Jordan responded, "Yeah, but there is in 'win'!"

I think Michael Jordan is right!

What he was telling his new coach and his teammates was this:

I am responsible. I am accountable. I will take the last shot with the game on the line. If I miss, I will take the heat in the pressroom from the reporters.

I will perform my job to the best of my ability. I will contribute to the success of my team and my teammates.

Michael Jordan understood that if he did his job as an individual, he would contribute to the success of the team. (And he did his job well enough to earn six World Championships!) Jordan also understood how to lift a team to a higher level of performance. He set the standard of individual commitment and dedication to success. He understood that if you put together a series of I's, you could put together a series of wins, achievements, and successes.

Each of us can embrace this principle today. The goal is to contribute to the betterment of the team by being the best I can be today. I am responsible. I am accountable. I will contribute my best efforts today.

Now, go sell somebody something!

THE ATTITUDE
OF GRATITUDE

Who gave you your first break? Was it an educator or coach, a Sunday school teacher, a boss, an associate?

Do you remember who had a positive impact early in your business career? What was his or her name? How did he contribute to your growth and development? What did she say that you really remember? How did he know that you needed to hear those exact words just at the right time?

Who came to your rescue when you needed it most? Who provided the arms to hold you, the ears to listen, and the heart to accept and not judge when you most needed it?

Who ventured out to rescue you and then brought you safely back to shore? Do you remember those people who helped you most in your life? Did you remember to thank them for their help? If you did not, you made a mistake.

It's not too late to thank them. Take the time TODAY to thank them. Thank them and express your gratitude. It's not too late to say, "Thanks." If you do not, you are making another mistake.

Now, go sell somebody something!

Prose for the Pros: Part II—It's a Great Day for Selling

Regardless of the weather, it is a great day for selling.

How successful will you be? There really is no telling!

It is a great day to go out and give it your best shot.

This is the kind of day to give it all you've got.

The prospects are there with their needs in plain sight.

Today you are so persuasive, they won't even put up a fight.

They will place orders and authorize contracts with glee.

Because today you will be the best that you can be.

It is a great day for selling and your slate is clean.

The day belongs to you, and all the lights are green!

You are ready for the day, for the whispers and the shouts.

You will be outrageously successful— there is no doubt!

It is a great day for selling, because this is true.

Today, like every day, your success depends on YOU!

So today, as you question, as you close, and as you strive.

Remember, it is a great day for selling, so KNOCK 'EM ALIVE!

Now, go sell somebody something!

IF YOU LOOK IN THE MIRROR, YOU MAY FIND YOU NEED A FAITH LIFT!

Have you ever been in an unfamiliar part of the city and running late for that BIG appointment? You take several wrong turns and you are lost! You pull into a convenience store and ask the clerk for directions. You finally get to the prospect's office and you start to doubt yourself. "Oh, no, this is the BIGGIE—competition is pulling out of the parking lot, and I can't blow this one! I hope this guy can't tell how nervous I am!"

Wait! Stop! Think! In that short period of time, do you realize that you placed more faith in the clerk who gave you directions than you have placed in yourself? Even though you don't know the person, you placed your confidence in him or her. Yet you begin to doubt someone you've known all your life—you!

Why do we do this to ourselves? Why do we continue to doubt ourselves, yet have so much faith in others?

In order to best serve your prospect today, you must have faith in yourself, your solutions, your company, and your support team. Starting today—right now—replace doubt with faith.

> Doubt sees the obstacles, Faith sees the way.
>
> Doubt sees the darkest night, Faith sees the day.
>
> Doubt dreads to take a step, but Faith soars on high.
>
> Doubt questions, "Who believes?" and Faith answers, "I!"

How do you do this? One way is to refer to the Victory List referred to in the chapter "Don't Miss the Good Life." Read a book, listen to a recording, focus on your past achievements. Accentuate the positive experiences in your life.

Give yourself a Faith Lift, beginning today!

Now, go sell somebody something!

Selling:
The Fun Profession

Here are two advertisements I ran across recently. The first one was a radio commercial for a local jewelry store. It went something like this: "We have the largest selection in town. If you don't see what you want in our store, there is an optometrist's office right next door!" I thought that would be a fun place to work.

The second ad was on the back of a delivery truck for a furniture company. The sign read: "Quality service since last Tuesday!" The owner of that company must have a great sense of humor.

Both these ads made me think the people employed there must enjoy their jobs.

Here are two serious lessons to learn from this:

1) Selling should be fun.

2) Selling should be enjoyable.

That's right. Selling should be fun. If you aren't having fun as a sales professional, you may be in the wrong business. Now, I know that selling isn't fun 100 percent of the time. However, it is a fun profession, and it should be mostly enjoyable.

As salespeople, we should acknowledge that our profession is FUN! I mean, what other professions allow us to have as much fun? You meet interesting people. You enjoy two-hour lunches. You solve other people's problems. You create problems for your sales support team. You win sales contests. You lose sales contests. You receive incorrect commission statements. You attempt to reconcile incorrect commission statements. Once a month, you get an expense check. You take direction from sales management. You second-guess sales management. Your mother-in-law doesn't think you have a real job. What a great profession!

If you aren't having fun as a salesperson at least three days a week, maybe you should rethink your career. Selling should be fun!

Here are a few ideas to remember as you enjoy your profession.

1. **Take yourself lightly.** Don't worry about what other people think. After all, they do it so rarely. Have fun and loosen up.

2. **Focus the attention off yourself.** Focus the attention where it belongs—on the prospect. When you get wrapped up in yourself, you have a small package. So, tune in to the prospect.

3. **Your prospect is more forgiving than you are.** Your prospect is not expecting a perfect sales call, just an effective one! Have fun and be effective.

4. **Employ the FIDO Principle.** When you make a mistake, you should shake off the dust. If the sales call doesn't achieve your desired results, it's okay. When this happens, employ the FIDO Principle: Forget It—Drive On. You are going to make a mistake now and then. It's okay. Learn from those mistakes and move on. Don't dwell on it. Have fun and don't major on minors.

5. **Remember to smile.** It increases your face value. Have fun and smile: enjoy the sales process as well as the sales victories.

Selling should be the most fun you can have between 8:00 in the morning and 5:15 in the afternoon.

Remember: Behind every successful salesman is a very surprised mother-in-law!

Now, go sell somebody something!

Definition of
a Professional

The great Hall of Fame baseball player Joe DiMaggio made everything look effortless. He was known as the "Yankee Clipper" because of his skill and grace. He once was asked why he played so hard. His reply was actually the secret of his greatness. He said, "I always thought there was at least one person in the stands who had never seen me play, and I didn't want to let them down."

His answer is also the definition of a true professional.

A true professional gives her best efforts day in and day out. A true professional invests daily in improving his skills. The sales professional makes each sales call count. The sales professional continually works on her "game." The sales professional seeks counsel and coaching from others who can assist in his development. The sales professional focuses on the needs of the prospect and seeks ways to solve those issues. The sales professional strives to draw out the best from those around her.

Today, give it your best shot. Today, make each sales interaction the most important one of your day. Today, focus on how you can strengthen your skills and techniques. Today, encourage your peers to be the best they can be.

Remember, today you may call on someone who has never seen you at your best . . . and you don't want to let them down.

Now, go sell somebody something!

Prose for the Pros: Part III—Look 'Em in the Eye As You Ask 'Em to Buy!

To be successful in selling, you don't have to prove you are smart.

You just have to show the prospect you have a lotta heart.

Don't get your foot in the door, though that's what's been said;

It's the wrong end of your body. Remember: Use your head.

Don't work without thinking, it causes a great deal of strain.

Work hard, plan, prioritize, and please, please use your brain.

Always have faith in yourself, never let your self-belief die—

As you look 'em in the eye and ask 'em to buy.

Now, go sell somebody something!

NEVER LEAVE
HOME WITHOUT IT

We all need it. We need it each and every day. Successful salespeople have it in abundance. Marginal performers have it; they just don't have enough of it! We all need to continue to develop it. What is it?

Stacy Dragila, world-record holder in the women's pole vault, claims it separates her from the rest of the field. Stacy says, "People ask me what I have that the other competitors don't have. Well, I just bring more confidence to the track than the rest of the girls." What was that? Confidence!

Confidence makes a difference. Confidence is a firm belief in yourself; it's a certainty or belief in one's own abilities. You may not have all the skills to accomplish a specific task at this present time, however, confidence gives you the assurance that you will be successful in the future. When you state that you are going to succeed in the future, you are not bragging . . . you are just telling the truth in advance!

Ted Williams had confidence. This Hall of Fame baseball player wanted to be known as the greatest hitter in baseball. His lifetime batting average of .344 and his 521 home runs certainly qualify him for that distinction. Ted had tremendous confidence. On his seventieth birthday, a sports writer asked, "Ted, if you were playing in today's game with the smaller ballparks and lack of quality pitching, what would you hit?" Without hesitating, Williams replied, "Oh, I'd hit about .320." The writer was taken aback; he quickly said, "But, Ted, you were the last player to hit .400, and your lifetime average is .344. And you think you'd only hit .320?"

Williams said, "Yeah, but I'm 70 years old!" Now that's confidence!

Confidence is maintaining faith in yourself—no matter what your age, sales situation, or product line, no matter what the economy is like.

Confidence. Never leave home without it.

Now, go sell somebody something!

How to Fill Your Cup Every Day

Y ou can fill your cup with all the good things that each sales day offers if you will just take the time to LEARN, LAUGH, and LOVE.

LEARN: You never learn enough about selling. There is always something else to learn or to improve upon in the field of selling. Perhaps it's how to listen more effectively, how to better manage your time or territory, or maybe how to network with other salespeople. Make sure you go to school today. Remember: School is never out for the pros!

LAUGH: Laughter is the shortest distance between two people. Find humor in today's sales interactions. In the Uncle Remus stories, Br'er Rabbit often spoke of his "laughing place." We all need to find our own personal "laughing place" and we need to visit it often. "What lies at the bottom of the ocean and twitches? A nervous wreck!" Don't become one. Laugh early and often. Don't take yourself too seriously.

LOVE: Love may not make the world go 'round, but it sure does make the trip worthwhile! Love is the most talked about and least understood subject in the world; however, there are some absolutes you can count on. Here are a few: Love is patient and kind, love is not jealous, it does not brag, and it is not proud. Love patiently accepts all things. It always trusts, always hopes, and always remains strong.

The most important thing in the world is to love someone. The second most important thing in the world is to be loved by someone else. The third most important thing is to have the first two things happen at the same time.

If you Learn and Laugh and Love today, you will have a full cup!

Now, go sell somebody something!

Avoid America's Favorite Pastime

What is America's favorite pastime?

Some people would have you think it is baseball. After all, it is called our National Pastime. True, many people attend all types of baseball games . . . from Little League to Major League. Many people think that baseball is a bit slow; someone said that baseball is fifteen minutes of action packed into three hours! Some people believe golf is the national pastime. Personally, I don't like to play golf because I stand too close to the ball—after I hit it!

There is another pastime that Americans are crazy about. Despite its popularity, this pastime should be avoided by all salespeople: it is called "transference of blame."

It is easy to blame others for our condition, our problems, and our state in life. We do it all the time.

"Mom, it isn't my fault I failed the test. You see, the teacher asked questions from the book! I thought they'd only be from his lectures!"

"Boss, it's not my fault the prospect didn't buy. I showed up at 1:45—for the 1:30 appointment!"

Of course, it's not our fault that we transfer the blame! No, sir. The people responsible for this are Adam and Eve. They started it all, and they are to blame. You remember, God asked Adam if he'd eaten the fruit. Adam said, "Lord, let me tell you about that woman you gave me." Eve said it was the serpent's fault. And, as you know, the snake didn't have a leg to stand on!

We are responsible for our thoughts and our actions. We are responsible for our hits and our misses. We are responsible for our successes and our mistakes. If others are responsible for our successes, then we need to invest in those people! We need to send them to school and to seminars so they become better educated. Once they are better, then we will get better. When they are successful, we will be successful.

But you know it doesn't work that way. We must stop blaming others. We must each stand on our own two feet and make our own way in the world. We need to avoid the pastime of "transference of blame." Take responsibility for your sales success today.

This ten-word, twenty-letter sentence says it all: "If it is to be, it is up to me!"

Now, go sell somebody something!

THANKS, MOM

My mother is ninety years old and she still goes to work every day at my brother's insurance company. She does take a long lunch break, but she's in the office each day; God has blessed her with excellent health. Recently a longtime customer asked Mom her age. When she told him, he said, "Mrs. Flanagan, I don't think I want to live to ninety." Mom replied, "That's because you aren't eighty-nine!" Mom is still quick.

Over the years, Mom has offered much sound advice and much wisdom. Here are a couple of her gems that have helped me through the years.

"I don't believe in divorce." Mom wasn't talking about marriage. She was referring to my eighth-grade teacher and me. Early in the school year, I wanted to switch history teachers. I told Mom and Dad that I had a personality conflict with my teacher (the teacher didn't think I had a person-ality—that was the conflict!). Therefore, I wanted Mom and Dad to help me change classes. Mom would have none of it. She said, "I don't believe in divorcing you from your teacher. You need to learn to solve this without your parents' help and with-out running away from the problem." That was cer-tainly good advice. I'm glad I followed it, because that teacher had a big impact on me and on my actually enjoying history. I also learned the impor-tance of "fight versus flight" when resolving inter-personal conflict. I learned to fight and not take the easy way out. This has certainly helped me in working through tough situations over the years. Thanks, Mom.

"You don't have to have the most points to be a winner." In my senior year of high school, our basketball team set a state record when we were beaten by the largest point margin in the history of the state tournament. We were beaten by forty-two points in the semifinals. (The man I guarded scored thirty-five points!) I was so depressed that I walked out of the locker room looking like the family pet had just died. I told my parents that I felt like a loser. As usual, Mom was there to unconditionally accept me and to cheer me up. She said, "Son, you're not looking at the entire picture. This is the first time in years that our school has gotten to the final four in the state playoffs. You have forgotten how hard you and your team worked and how much you've sacrificed to get this far. You are a not a loser to me. You don't have to have the most points on the scoreboard to be a winner." Wow! Just what I needed to hear. Later in my life, I often use that truism in dealing with my sales career. I can make a good, solid sales call, yet not get the order. However, if I consider the entire picture, I can still feel good about myself, my sales skills, and the effort I put forth. Thanks, Mom.

Now, go sell somebody something!

PROSE FOR THE PROS: PART IV—USE YOUR HEAD

If your attitude is down and you don't think you can do it,

When you've just left an account thinking you really blew it,

Don't make another call. Go straight home and go to bed.

'Cause more sales are lost not in the prospect's office

But in the salesperson's head!

Now, go sell somebody something!

JUST BE YOU

Someone once said, "To be successful as a sales professional, you need to be as aggressive as Donald Trump, as innovative as Albert Einstein, as independent as Katharine Hepburn, as analytical as Sherlock Holmes, as funny as Bill Cosby, as poised as Cary Grant, and as driven as Hillary Clinton, with a smile that rivals Meg Ryan's!"

NOT SO! You just have to be **you!**

You were hired because of *your* values, beliefs, and convictions. You weren't hired to be someone else. The only element you offer your clients that is totally exclusive is *you!*

You should use this to your advantage. YOU are the only unique sales advantage that you have each and every time you face a competitor. You should communicate that unique advantage each time you interact with your prospects.

There are five reasons people don't buy from you. Here are the first four: no want, no need, no hurry, and no money. As a professional salesperson you deal with those every day of your sales career. The fifth reason is the most difficult to overcome. The fifth reason more people don't buy from you is no trust! You build trust by being yourself. You win a person's confidence by being consistent over a period of time. You win people over by sharing and exhibiting your values, beliefs, and convictions with them.

You've had years, maybe decades of practice being yourself. Use that practice to your advantage.

Now, go sell somebody something!

YES, YOU CAN!

My wife and I enjoy going to the movies. Often we go with another couple, Doug and Wendy. Several years ago, before the theaters sold bottled water, there was always a dilemma when we got to the concession stand. You see, Wendy enjoys popcorn, but she doesn't like carbonated drinks. So this was the scene at the counter: The teenage worker would ask Doug what he'd like. Doug would say, "I'd like a popcorn, a soft drink, and a cup of ice, which I will fill with tap water."

Well, this was out of the ordinary, so the youngster would say, "Sir, I'm sorry, I can't do that."

Doug would respond, "Yes, you can. I will pay for the cup of ice." When Doug detected some hesitation, he would simply lean forward, smile and say, "Yes, you can!"

The young man or woman would then reach over, grab a cup, fill it with ice, and give it to Doug. Doug would then pay for the cup of ice, gather up his drink and popcorn, and off we'd go to the movie.

There is a great lesson here. Sometimes you just need to be told: "Yes, you can!"

There are people in your organization who believe you can do it. After all, those people hired you, invested time to train you, explained the product line to you, and answered as many of your questions as they could. They believe you can.

You believe in yourself, don't you? Of course you do. You believed in yourself to purchase this book. (Unless you borrowed this book and have no intention of returning it to the owner!)

Sometimes you just need to be reminded that you can. So let me remind you: YES, YOU CAN!

Now, go sell somebody something!

THE FIRST DAY OF THE REST OF YOUR LIFE

If this really is the first day of the rest of your life, you should strive to make it your best ever! How do you achieve this? One way is to GIVE. That's right, give. Giving is the key to a successful future in any endeavor, especially in sales. Here's what I mean: since it is more blessed to give than to receive, we should give away something every day.

What do you give away? Here are a few suggestions:

Begin by giving away your smiles! Do you realize that between the first and last letters of "smiles" there is a "mile" of good? This is painless, it costs nothing, and it may be priceless to the receiver. Your smile is one of the strongest forces on earth. It can lighten the load, it can brighten a gloomy afternoon, it can pick up a two-hundred-pound man who is down, and it can move people to action. If you are happy, tell your face. And then give away one of your smiles to someone who really needs it. You'll be glad you did.

Give away your ears? I said GIVE AWAY YOUR EARS! How? By listening, really listening. My wife says I am not a good communicator because I don't listen very well. (At least, I think that's what she said.) Two points about listening: First, good listeners are given credit for intelligence they don't necessarily possess! Second, if you don't listen to your loved ones, they will find someone who will!

Give away black marks on paper. Take out a sheet of paper and write a thank-you note or an I-appreciate-you note to someone. Tell a child, a business associate, a friend, a spouse, a loved one, a parent, or a client that you appreciate and value them. Write your thoughts down and then set the note on his or her desk, chair, mailbox, briefcase, or suitcase. Yes, e-mails are good, but a handwritten note is certainly more treasured by the receiver.

In summary, give away your smiles, give away your ears by listening, and give away your gratitude by taking the time and effort to handwrite a sincere note of appreciation. If you do these things, you will most assuredly make this the best first day of the rest of your life, and maybe of someone else's life, too.

Now, go sell somebody something!

Lessons Learned from our National Pastime

Whether we are fans or not, we can learn a lot from the game of baseball. Here are some important lessons that baseball teaches us:

Baseball is a simple game. In baseball, it's the number of times you reach home safely that counts. Now that's simple. Sales success doesn't require twelve moving parts and a complex system. Oftentimes we try to complicate life, our sales career, and our relationships. Keep it simple. In its simplest form, selling is a communication process, and successful salespeople keep the process simple.

Good things happen when you work hard.

Effort is rewarded in the game of baseball, as it is in the game of sales. In baseball, the players are taught to "run out every ground ball." They are urged to "play all nine innings." On the offensive side of the game, players are told "make every at-bat count." In sales, we are taught that every prospect is a potential customer. Each prospect we meet is important. We should make each sales call count; we should never pass up an opportunity to establish trust and rapport. Make each sales contact meaningful.

Not everyone can win a World Series, but everyone can have a World Series attitude. Ernie Banks is a great example of this. He is known as "Mr. Cub" for his successful years with the Chicago Cubs. Yet, at one time, Ernie held the record for playing the most games without winning a championship. Did that hurt his attitude? No! Ernie was known for his positive attitude, his love of the game, and his favorite expression: "LET'S PLAY TWO!" What a great attitude and what a positive example for all of us. You may not win every sale, but you can have a winner's attitude.

You can't steal second if your foot is on first base. There are no rewards without some risks. We must take chances to gain success. We must move out of our comfort zone and apply for that position, make a call on that tough prospect, meet new people, try new sales techniques, ask those tough questions.

Learn from these baseball lessons and you'll increase your chances for sales success.

Now, go sell somebody something!

WHO HELPED YOU BUILD YOUR DREAM MACHINE?

Y̶ou couldn't build it on your own: you needed help. Your ideas and blueprints needed other ideas, insights, and input. New ideas get together and mingle with your old ideas. They then produce more ideas and blueprints. They expand your thinking, and your ideas get bigger and better.

We're talking about DREAMS—your dreams! Who helped you build your dreams? Was it a parent, spouse, friend, coach, teacher, boss, co-worker? Did he serve as an encourager? Did she put wings to your dreams? Did she communicate ways to achieve those dreams?

George MacIntyre helped me. He was an older fraternity brother who was a salesman for the IBM Corporation. When he visited the fraternity house, he looked like he was having fun and enjoying the sales profession. He encouraged me to apply for my first position at IBM. Another was Reverend Bob Richards, Olympic medalist and motivational speaker. He was the first motivational speaker I heard. He made a huge impression on me. Obviously, Zig Ziglar had a positive impact on me, and that impact continues to this very day.

These are some of the people who helped me build my Dream Machine. They encouraged me, they counseled me, they guided me. I'm very grateful they cared enough to invest time and effort in me.

Reminders:

1. Continue to build your Dream Machine.

2. Help others build their Dream Machines.

3. Give others permission to dream and be successful.

4. Give yourself permission to continue to dream.

5. Take a few minutes in the next day or two to thank someone who assisted you in your dreams.

Dreams do come true—for those who dream!

Now, go sell somebody something!

SALES LEVITY

The board of a huge conglomerate decided it would expand its hiring practices. Subsequently, the company hired several cannibals. Each cannibal attended the new employee orientation. They were exposed to all the courses each new employee was given. They were given all the benefits the firm had to offer; however, they were told in no uncertain terms that they were not allowed to eat any of their fellow employees. Each cannibal agreed to that stipulation.

Several weeks later, the human resource director noticed that one of the administrative assistants had disappeared. She approached the cannibals, but they all claimed to know nothing about the disappearance.

When the director left, the leader of the cannibals turned to the others and said, "Which one of you ate the administrative assistant?" A hand went up. The leader screamed, "You idiot! For weeks we've been eating the salespeople and not one person noticed. But you ruined it all by eating someone important!"

Now, go sell somebody something!

STOP! LOOK!
AND CELEBRATE!

Success in sales requires a great deal of dedication and commitment. You must dedicate yourself each and every day to put forth the effort that success demands. You must commit to do those things that lead to victories as a professional salesperson. And once you land the sale, you should Stop! Look! And Celebrate!

That's right, you need to celebrate your victories. It is a very competitive marketplace that you enter each day. Your sales victories are hard won and require a great deal of effort to achieve. As a professional salesperson, you work at solving a prospect's problems. You expend the effort to identify the challenges and then offer solutions to those challenges. And very often you save your prospects money along the way! When you are successful, you deserve to celebrate your victory!

This doesn't mean you take the rest of the afternoon off! It doesn't mean that you get cocky and kick your feet up on your desk for the remainder of the week.

It does mean that you stop and analyze what you did to solidify that sale. It means that you look back at the sales call and take note of the steps, activities, questions, and strategies that enabled you to identify the prospect's needs. Then you have every right to celebrate the results of your efforts! The key is to celebrate immediately following your victory so that you can savor the moment. Celebrate while you are still sweating! By doing so, you will want to capture more moments just like this one. The best time to make a call is directly after you've made a sale! Success breeds success! So, while you are celebrating, you should walk to the next prospective customer, introduce yourself, and ask him if he'd like to take advantage of all the benefits your firm has to offer.

Remember: Stop! Look! And Celebrate!

Now, go sell somebody something!

SMILE—IT INCREASES YOUR FACE VALUE

S alespeople need to smile more; however, often-times we have to be reminded to do so.

What makes you smile? Is it your children? Seeing an old friend? Having a prospect actually return your phone call? Holding hands with your spouse as you walk in the mall?

Here are some reminders of what you might consider happy times. I hope they bring a smile to your face.

The first date with your spouse.

What you told your best friend after that first date.

Your last year of high school.

Your favorite high school teacher.

Having someone laugh at your joke.

Remembering to tell that joke again.

Your first car.

Paying off your present car.

Your child's first day of school.

Your child's last day of college.

You and your spouse's special song.

Your spouse actually remembering the name of that song.

If you need a smile today, you may want to find your wedding album. Or you may want to locate the pictures of your family's first vacation.

Keep smiling.

Keep smiling.

Now, go sell somebody something!

DON'T MISS THE GOOD LIFE

I f you don't like where you are at this time in your life, rest assured you aren't stuck there. There are ways to move past this spot. Let's explore three ways to do just that.

1. You are what you are and where you are because of what has gone into your mind. You can change what you are and you can change where you are by changing what goes into your mind. How do you achieve this?

One way is to begin a listening and/or reading program. For just minutes a day, you can feed your mind with the pure, the powerful, and the positive. How? Turn off the radio and play motivational and inspirational tapes and CDs. Remember "Automobile University?" Enroll! Give yourself that checkup from the neck up!

2. **Learn from successful failures.** That's right, learn from those who made every effort—and failed. Learn from baseball Hall of Famer Reggie Jackson: He hit over five hundred home runs in his big league career, yet he struck out close to twenty-five hundred times! He didn't put the ball in play twenty-five hundred times. However, he didn't stop swinging for the fences.

Abraham Lincoln failed in most endeavors he tried. Yet, as the sixteenth President of the United States, he successfully led our nation in some of her darkest moments!

The lesson to be learned is this: don't give up . . . keep swinging!

3. **Keep a "victory list."** You should make a list—both mentally and physically—to remind yourself of past successes. This will fuel your motivation by reminding you that you *can do it!* Your self-worth will be enhanced and your confidence will be increased; we salespeople need all we can of those elements. This list can include things from childhood to the present.

You will find that by making this list you will recall that you possess all the qualities and attributes necessary for success.

Well, there you have it. Three hints on how to get "unstuck." By implementing these ideas, you will become more dangerous than you are now!

Now, go sell somebody something!

Prose for the Pros: Part V—Food for Thought

H ere are some thoughts to chew on at lunch. I hope you enjoy them.

The only time you can't afford to fail
is the last time you try!

The best mirror is a friend's eye.

You cannot climb the ladder of success with your hands in your pockets.

A fool and his money are soon parted. But how did they get together in the first place?

Don't pray for lighter burdens;
pray for a stronger back.

There is no traffic jam
on the extra mile.

Failure is the foundation of success.

When selling yourself, remember to
believe in your product!

Kindness is one thing you can never
give away—it always comes back.

If your day is hemmed with prayer,
it is less likely to unravel.

Selling is nothing more than a
"transference of feeling."

Use the talents that you have. The
woods would be very quiet if no birds
sang except those that sang best!

Now, go sell somebody something!

SCHOOL IS NEVER OUT
FOR THE PROFESSIONAL!

A lady said to her elderly pastor, "Reverend, I have attended church services for over forty years. I have heard over fifteen hundred sermons, but I can't remember a single one of them. Perhaps you preachers should spend your time in a more worthy pursuit."

The pastor replied, "I have been married more than forty years. My wife has prepared over twenty-five thousand meals. I can't remember the menu of any of them, but nonetheless, I have been nourished by each one. I pray that she will continue in this most worthy pursuit."

Even though we can't remember everything we read, hear, or see, to say we should not continue to learn would be foolish. We live in a time when opportunities for acquiring knowledge are endless. More books are on shelves than ever before. The Internet has set education right in front of us, around the clock. More instructional tapes are available than at any time in our history. More campuses offer continuing education than ever; there are more seminars scheduled in your city each week than you could possibly attend.

In spite of this abundance of available knowledge, many of us are sadly undereducated. This is not simply a lack of learning; it is also a lack of initiative. Fred Smith claims that it is okay not to have a degree; it is not okay to be uneducated. This is our responsibility.

Admiral Hyman Rickover said that if America is to survive, it must fight against ignorance and mediocrity. "A free society can survive only through men and women of integrity. Mediocrity can destroy us, just as surely as perils far more famous." Admiral Rickover issued this warning: "I believe it is the duty of each of us to act as if the fate of the world depended on our actions, because in a society that is willing to accept mediocrity, the opportunities for failure are boundless."

The pursuit of knowledge makes learning a continuum. When we cease to learn, we cease to grow! Self-improvement should be our constant goal. It is a most worthy pursuit.

Now, go sell somebody something!

SEEK BALANCE IN ALL AREAS OF LIFE

Several years ago I had one of those days that all salespeople have. I came home at 7:30 p.m. with still more paperwork to complete. My wife had left a plate of food on the table for me. I stuffed food down my throat for about five minutes, then called out, "I have work to do. I will be in the study." I went back to our study, opened my briefcase, and dived into the work. About five minutes later, my seven-year-old son came hurrying down the hall and bounded into my study. He was excited! He held up his glove and baseball and said, "Daddy, it's still light outside. Can we play catch tonight?" I took a deep breath and said, "Patrick, I'm sorry, but I've got work to do." I thought that had gotten rid of him, but it hadn't. He still stood in the doorway but his smile had been replaced by a frown; he had tears in his eyes. He walked out of the study and into the kitchen and asked, "Mom, why can't Daddy play with me tonight?"

Cyndi looked down and suggested, "Daddy couldn't get all of his work done at the office."

Patrick looked back and said, "Well, why don't they put him in a slower group?"

With all our daily challenges, we salespeople often feel like we are in a "slower group." This causes us to lose focus on our priorities, and we fall out of balance. When this happens, it is usually our family that suffers the most. There is an old saying that, "Love means sharing the best years of your life with those who make them the best years of your life." We can't achieve this if we are continually out of balance.

How balanced are you in your personal, professional, and family lives? Do you find yourself sacrificing one for the other? Well, it is an easy rut to get into. While there is no one absolute solution for this, here are a couple of ideas that can contribute to maintaining a more balanced life.

Arrange your priorities. Most of our priorities fall into one of six categories: family, spiritual, physical, career/financial, social, and mental. You have to determine the importance of each one. A friend shared with me that he didn't take up golf (physical and social priorities) until the last of his three children (family priority) was in college.

Another way to reach balance is to communicate with your loved ones. Let them know that this week you will be working late on Tuesday and Wednesday nights. However, the rest of the week you will be home in time for meals, running the car pool after practice, and assisting with homework assignments.

Maintaining a balanced life requires a great deal of commitment and dedication; however, if you learn to do it, the results will prove invaluable to you and to your loved ones!

Now, go sell somebody something!

The Psychology
of Closing

The closing stage of the sales process should be the logical conclusion of your selling efforts. However, some sales professionals develop anxiety when entering this stage.

By the time you reach the closing stage, the most difficult part of the sales process has been completed. A sports analogy may help explain this. In baseball, getting to third base and not reaching home safely is frustrating. But, if you think about it, getting to third base means the base runner has done several things well. He reached first base safely. He made his way to second base and now he is on third base. He is in a position to obtain his objective.

The same is true in selling. You have worked all this time to get into a position to help the customer "reach home safely" and to obtain your objective; that is, to solve his problem and have him or her receive value from your solution.

Why does the closing stage cause so much anxiety? Here are four possible reasons.

1. **Fear of Rejection:** All salespeople have to face this dilemma. However, there is a simple way to solve this: separate rejection from refusal. They are different. One is personal (rejection) and the other is professional (refusal). We shouldn't take a business refusal personally. Here is the reason: there are only a half dozen or so people in the entire world that can put you down personally. In my case, there are only six people: my mother, my wife, my two children, my brother, and my sister. If none of these labels fits you, you can't put me down. Oh, you can refuse to purchase from me, but that is business refusal, not personal rejection. I've learned many times over that your opinion of me on a sales call in the morning doesn't determine my family's opinion of me at night. I've also learned that your opinion of me during a sales call doesn't determine my opinion of myself after the sales call! If you say no to my sales recommendation,

I'm going to take that as a business refusal, not as a personal putdown. As a professional, I must work on my selling skills . . . but I still have dignity and value as a person.

2. **Fear that the Product Will Not Meet Expectations:** You must know your product offerings so well that you can link the features and functions to the customer's expected value. If you know that your product does not meet his or her expectations, you should cease your selling efforts, thank the customer for meeting with you, and excuse yourself. Any town is too small to establish a reputation for being a salesperson who pushes products on customers. However, if you are certain the product can meet expectations, you should proceed with all your skills to demonstrate the benefits to your customer. Remember: To be convincing, you must first be convinced. You must have confidence in your sales abilities, the capabilities of your product, and the value your product offers the customer.

3. **Uncertainty about When to Close:** We teach that selling is a process, not an event. Once again, closing is something you do *with* the customer, not *to* the prospect. Therefore, if you have a clear process that is focused on the customer, you will know where you are in the

process as well as where the customer is in the process. If you and the prospect are both at the closing stage, you should have full confidence to ask for the order. If the customer is still in the stage of understanding his or her needs, you need to complete that stage before asking for the order. Closing the sale is not an adversarial stage of the process. The closing is a joint effort between you and the customer, which assists the customer in reaching his or her goals of solving problems and moving forward. When you and the prospect reach this stage together, you should confidently ask for the order.

4. **Fear of Losing:** What happens when you ask for the order and you get it? You win! But, what happens when you ask for the order and you don't get it? (Be careful with your answer; this is a trick question! And this was covered very early in the book. Do you remember?) If you don't get the order, you do not lose—you break even! That's right. You don't lose, you break even! Part of your job description as a sales professional is to ask people to exchange their money for your products and services. You are doing your job when you ask for the order. No one can get mad at you when you do your job. Oh, you have to do your job correctly, but you are simply doing your job well when you ask

for the order. And you can't lose when you are doing your job well.

So there you have it. Four reasons for experiencing a bit of anxiety at the closing stage of the selling process—and for letting go of that anxiety. Remember to believe in yourself and your product, and ask for the order at the right time. After all, that's your job!

Now, go sell somebody something!

MENTAL SNACKS

Here are some thoughts to toss around tonight as you and your spouse are sharing a meal. I hope they are encouraging to you.

Regardless of your past, your
future is a clean slate!

Seconds count,
especially when dieting.

People are more important
than projects.

He who can't be counseled
can't be helped.

Children need more models
and fewer critics.

Troubles are like babies—they
grow bigger if you nurse them.

Building boys is easier
than mending men.

After God created the world, He
created man and woman. Then to
keep the whole thing from falling
apart, He created humor.

Your children need your presence
more than your presents.

Despite the cost of living,
it is still very popular.

A person may not be as good as
you tell him he is, but he'll try
harder afterward.

We are all richer than
we think we are.

Now, go sell somebody something!

Lessons Learned from the Good Book

We should all read the Bible on a daily basis; it teaches so many wonderful things. There are many benefits to doing so; it will help us now and it will take the heat off us later!

One of my favorite stories is from 1 Samuel in the Old Testament. In the seventeenth chapter, we learn a great deal about positive thinking, setting goals, and taking action on our dreams. And we learn all these lessons from a teenager named David.

David's brothers were fighting for the army of Israel against the dreaded Philistine army. David's father told him to deliver a "care package" of corn and bread to his brothers and some cheese to the captain. This particular morning, the nine-foot-tall, four hundred-pound Goliath was again challenging the army of Israel. David heard of three different rewards for the man who killed this giant. He heard that King Saul was granting great riches, and the princess's hand in marriage, and exemption from taxes for life! Well, these were great incentives for David.

He ran and told his brothers that he was up for the challenge. His positive attitude made them angry, and they said, "The giant is too big to hit!" But David's positive attitude said, "No, the giant is too big to miss!" So off he went to sign up for the fight. The king tried to give him a suit of armor. David tried it on, but it did not fit his plan. You see, David had faced challenges like this in the past, and he had formed a plan. His plan was to use his slingshot. Well, you probably know the rest of the story. David took the rock and rolled the giant. (This could be the first hint of "rock and roll"—but that's another story.)

David won the battle for several reasons: first and foremost, David's attitude was very positive. You see, he was not comparing his size to Goliath's size. His attitude was to compare Goliath to the size of God. That was a mismatch right there!

Second, David was prepared: he had chosen five smooth, flat river rocks. (His plan was to have a few stones in reserve, in case he ran into any objections.) David also had an incentive, a goal, a motivator. He'd never had riches or a princess's hand in marriage; those are worthwhile goals.

Finally, David was action oriented. For forty days, the giant had challenged the professional soldiers of the army of Israel. For forty days no action had been taken. On David's first day on the job, he took positive action and "closed a sale."

We should all follow David's example. Choose a goal, list the rewards, maintain a positive attitude, and take action! Good luck with slaying your giants today.

Now, go sell somebody something!

YOU AND THE GOLDEN GATE BRIDGE

Follow me on this one. I am going to make a comparison between you and the Golden Gate Bridge in San Francisco, California. The analogy is a good one to use in the sales profession. At the conclusion, I hope you will think about this comparison often.

Here are some facts about the Golden Gate Bridge. It was first opened to traffic on May 28, 1937. It is known as one of the "Seven Wonders of the Modern World." It was built to withstand a huge traffic load. In the year 2002, the annual revenue generated by tolls on the bridge was $59,289,000! That's a lot of quarters.

The annual traffic in fiscal year 2002 was 40,694,792 vehicles. The monthly load on the Golden Gate Bridge was 3,391,233. That equates to a total of 111,493 vehicles each and every day for an entire year. WOW! This is truly an engineering marvel. The engineers who designed this structure were pretty smart.

Now, here is the point: The Golden Gate Bridge was designed to handle the traffic load—in increments: if you were to put the annual load of forty million vehicles on the bridge at the same time, it would collapse under the weight. The bridge was not designed to handle that type of load. If you were to put the entire monthly load of 3.4 million vehicles on the bridge at the same time, it would collapse under the weight. The bridge was not designed to handle that weight all at once: the bridge was designed to handle one day's traffic at a time. So are we!

It is important, even vital, that we plan our sales year, our sales quarter, our sales month, and our sales day. By so doing, we have a better chance of achieving our sales goals. However, we have to handle our sales career one day at a time—otherwise, we will collapse under the weight.

Now, go sell somebody something!

A HOUSE IS NOT A HOME

When my wife and I purchased our first new house, we were so excited that we told everyone. After signing the papers, I was telling everyone what a nice house it was and how Cyndi and I looked forward to moving in, planting grass and shrubs, maintaining the landscape, and all the stuff that goes into a first house.

My sales partner at the time was a veteran salesman named Jim Raff. He was very experienced and knowledgeable in many areas. He had always given me useful advice about selling, dealing with customers, managing your manager, and many other things. Jim and his wife Jackie had been married for many years and had five children. Of all the talks we had over the years, the advice he gave me about my new home meant the most.

He sat me down in the coffee shop and offered me what I call "a house isn't a home . . . unless you make it so" advice. Jim talked about the houses he had owned in the past and what he had learned from them. I was twenty-four years old at the time, so I was something of a novice in this area. Jim wrote on a napkin in big, bold letters: POET. Of course I was curious, so I asked him where this was going and what POET meant.

He said that he had seen many neighbors over the years who took better care of their houses than they did their homes. He admitted that even he had been guilty of that, at times. He said that oftentimes we spend much time and effort on the outside of our houses, but neglect the inside of our homes. He cited examples of homeowners who were more concerned with winning the neighborhood's "yard of the month" contest than with winning the love of the people who lived inside that house!

He had used POET for some time now, and it seemed to have worked well for him and his family. He said, "P O E T stands for 'Put Off Every Thing' and be there for your family." He reminded me that sales is a very demanding profession. It constantly takes you away from your family and makes great demands on your time. He encouraged me to develop the habit of "putting off everything and taking care of my family." He emphasized that the work will always be waiting for you the next day at the office; your family needs you now. Therefore, POET. Put off everything and take care of what's on the inside of your house.

Over the years that advice has served me well. I have learned a couple of other things along those lines. If you are a mom or a dad, here are two other ideas that you can use to ensure that you invest more in your home than your house.

DEAR: Drop Everything And Read. (This is especially true if you have younger children.) Anyone in the family can call "DEAR" at any time and every family member must stop whatever they are doing and pick up a book and read. If the children are young, then Mom and Dad may have to read to them.

DEAL: Drop Everything And Listen. This is very similar to the "DEAR" process. This could occur at the dinner table: each family member gets an opportunity to tell what happened during his or her day. The rest of the family must listen until each family member has finished sharing.

These suggestions allow you to build the inside of your home. They also allow you to build memories that you, your spouse, and your children can cherish for years to come.

If you care for your home, the house will take care of itself!

Now, go sell somebody something!

There's Magic
in Enthusiasm

Nothing great ever happens without enthusiasm.

Enthusiasm is the difference between competing and winning.

When a word is overused, it can lose its power and its meaning. Enthusiasm can be just that type of word. However, when we study enthusiasm, we can capture its true meaning and therefore recapture its power! Enthusiasm has nothing to do with jumping and shouting. That's hysteria, and hysteria is giving enthusiasm a bad name.

The origin of "enthusiasm" is in the Greek root words "en theos," meaning "the god within." Therefore, this powerful word is really an internal feeling. In his book, *See You at the Top*, Zig Ziglar uses an acrostic to describe the power of the last four letters of the word "enthusiasm": I Am Sold Myself. If you accept the "God within" principle and if you are sold on yourself, then you are well on your way to being enthusiastic. This leads you to an outward expression of inner feelings. When this happens, you become a very effective sales professional. I will give you a magic formula for leading a more enthusiastic life. If you implement these action steps, you will feel the magic.

First, ACTIVATE your motivators. Why are you in the world of sales? Why are you making those contacts, those phone calls, and investing in prospecting activities? Remember what motivates you, and then activate those motivators.

Second, ANALYZE what you need to do or what you need to learn, in order to become more successful. Once you have realized that you never graduate from selling, you need to invest in those areas that will assist you in performing your sales activities more effectively. By developing your skills, you will act more confidently and more enthusiastically.

Third, take ACTION! Remember, logic will not change an emotion, but action will! Successful people make a habit of taking action on those things that unsuccessful people fail to do.

So there you have the magic of enthusiasm: ACTI-VATE your motivators, ANALYZE what you need to improve upon, and take ACTION.

Yes, you are absolutely correct: this is certainly not magic. It gets back to following the steps necessary for success. I enthusiastically encourage you to "grow git 'em" today!

Now, go sell somebody something!

PREPARE FOR
YOUR FUTURE

(After all, you are going to spend the
rest of your life there!)

The best way to invest in your future is to create it! That's right. You can create your future if you take the time to plan, design, and create meaningful goals that prepare you for your tomorrows. Here are four simple, straightforward hints on setting goals.

Make no small plans, for they have no capacity to stir men's souls! Therefore, your goals must be big! It requires a big goal to create the excitement for accomplishment.

Others can stop you temporarily—you are the only one who can do it permanently. Without long range goals, you are likely to be overcome by short-term frustration. Long range goals continually motivate you to move forward.

If you expect to achieve your major goals, you must be willing to work toward them on a daily basis. What separates a goal from a dream? The answer: You are a goal setter if you are working toward your goal every single day.

Become a meaningful specific rather than a wondering generality. You must harness your energies and focus on specific activities that drive you toward your goal.

Well, there you have it. These four hints will get you started creating your future. It is important to plan your future because if you don't, someone else will!

Now, go sell somebody something!

THE EMPATHY ATTITUDE

I n order to build your sales career, you must have
the ego drive to succeed. However, that personal
ego drive must be balanced with empathy for your
prospects and customers.

Many salespeople do not recognize the difference
between empathy and sympathy and how to apply
them in the world of selling. Empathy means you
understand how your prospect feels, although you
do not feel the same way. Sympathy means that
you feel the same way as your prospect feels.

Example: On a cruise ship, suppose you see a fellow
passenger leaning over the rail suffering from sea-

sickness. Sympathy is hanging over the rail with him because you feel the same way! Empathy is when you understand how the passenger feels, so you offer a seasickness pill.

Empathy allows you to step back from the problem, clearly focus on it, and assist in solving it.

Empathy is an essential ingredient to your sales success. You recognize the problem, you understand how the prospect feels, and you offer solutions to the problem. If you know how the prospect thinks and feels, you are going to sell more because you can communicate more effectively to his or her needs.

It is important not to confuse your situation with your prospect's situation and vice versa. Remember, your needs, wants, desires, and capacity to pay have no bearing on your prospect's needs, wants, desires, and capacity to pay.

You have to know your products, your sales abilities, and the prospect's needs so well that you can sell through his or her eyes. That's the value of empathy—that's the way to build your sales career.

Now, go sell somebody something!

THE LIGHTER SIDE OF SELLING: SALESPEOPLE DO WEIRD THINGS

I asked several of my clients to submit weird things that salespeople do. Well, they responded with some strange stuff. Here is a sampling of the responses:

"Our president is very sales-focused. He gets excited about making sales. He challenged the entire sales team to reach a certain goal. If we reached it, he would run around the building in just his boxer shorts!" (I suggested that this salesperson bring his camera to work. Photos like that may help at his next performance review!)

"When I worked at a western clothing store, I noticed an increase in sales volumes according to the phases of the moon. Sales tended to increase from new moon to full moon. I tried to take advantage of this 'full-moon buying impulse.' I could clear out old stock that had been sitting around for years!" (Yeah, but it was hard to sell with all that howling going on!)

"I am in the car business. Our sales manager challenged us to make buyers get in the trunk of the car. If we did, he'd give us a cash bonus. It was an easy $50 for me!" (Was this by chance a Mafia-owned dealership?)

"I sell sponsorships for a top university football program. I always carry a football with me to client meetings. Sometimes we toss the ball in the office to create rapport, or I will toss the ball to see if the client can catch it. Some think this is a weird idea; however, this is what I am known for." (It's a good thing he doesn't sell Volkswagens!)

"Before making a sales call, I write down on my talking pad in big, bold print '70/30.' It reminds me to listen seventy percent of the time." (Funny, when I get home my wife does the same thing to me!)

Well, there you have it. Weird stuff that salespeople do. These things are what keep our profession lively and salespeople energized.

Now, go sell somebody something!

SAY YES! TO GOALS

Here are some random thoughts on goals and goal setting. I hope you can use them to inspire you to set and attain your goals this year.

> You seldom hit anything unless you shoot at it.

> It is useless to carry the ball until you know where the goal line is located.

> There is no sense aiming for a goal when you have no arrow in your bow.

> If you don't plan your future, someone else will.

> Failure is not missing the goal. Failure is aiming too low.

A genius is a person who shoots at something no one else sees and hits it.

If you don't know where you are going, you may miss it when you get there!

Your life can't go according to plan if you have no plan.

People are like thumbtacks. They are useful if they have a good head and are pointed in the right direction.

Success has little to do with speed but much to do with direction.

The world can certainly use more vision and less television.

Now, go sell somebody something!

THE MARK OF
A PROFESSIONAL

S everal centuries ago in medieval England, towns-people wore clothing to indicate their positions in life. Their clothing also indicated their wealth, their status within the community, and their guild. In other words, these "markings" indicated their professions. The distinctions appeared most often in the hoods that townspeople wore and the color of those hoods. Laws were passed to prevent commoners from dressing "out of rank," that is, to keep commoners and merchants from dressing like the nobility. Apparently some people would wear a colored hood that increased their status. Laws were passed to prevent these hoods from being falsely worn, hence, the term "falsehood."

This leads to some interesting questions about the sales profession: What indicates your professionalism to the outside world? What are you "wearing" to distinguish yourself as a professional salesperson? How will others recognize that you are a professional? Here are some elements that will indicate your professionalism. Try them on for size:

Show up. Show up on time. Show up, show up on time, and show up dressed to play. Let's explore each of these.

Show up! A professional salesperson realizes that a solid work ethic is essential for success. You must work both hard and smart each day. As Woody Allen says, "80 percent of success is showing up!" You must be present to win!

Show up. Show up on time! A sales professional understands the importance of being punctual and values time, both for self and for others. No one wants to earn a reputation for being late for meetings, appointments, or other events. Professionals separate themselves from others by being timely in all aspects of sales activities and behaviors.

Show up. Show up on time. Show up dressed to play. A sales professional understands that this element addresses not just appearance but also preparation. Yes, your appearance is important. The key is to dress appropriately for your sales environment. This also means to be prepared for your sales day, each sales call, and any unsuspected opportunities that may arise. One more time: you must remember that preparation compensates for any deficiency in talent!

Well, there you have it: three marks of a professional salesperson. Show up. Show up on time. Show up dressed to play. If you "wear" these each day, you'll indicate to others that you are a true professional.

Now, go sell somebody something!

FOUNDATION BLOCKS FOR YOUR SALES CAREER

Webster's Dictionary defines "foundation" as "the basis or ground work of anything; that on which any thing stands, and by which it is supported." Our sales careers should be built on a firm, solid foundation. Here are five building blocks to include in your sales career's foundation:

Don't try to be perfect. Your prospects do not want to be part of a sales interview where the salesperson is striving for perfection. It is going to waste the prospect's time and make him or her mad. Your prospects don't expect perfection on a sales call. They do demand that you be effective on a sales call! Therefore, take the pressure off yourself. Don't strive to be perfect. Strive to be effective.

Choose to acquire an optimistic outlook. Do you realize that fear and faith have the same definition? That's right, the same definition. Here is the definition: believing what you can't see will happen! If that's the case, we should develop an optimistic, upbeat attitude in all that we do. Since fear and faith have the same definition, choose faith!

Don't worry. Worry only causes harm. This foundation block is biblical! It is a paraphrase of Psalm 37:8: worrying is harmful. It always results in some type of waste: your time, your attitude, your mood, or your friendships. Worrying occurs between rumor and fact; don't make a decision until all the facts are in. Once you have the facts, you can choose the solution; *then* you can choose your emotion!

Be prepared for change. Everyone is in favor of progress; not everyone is in favor of change. Yet you can't have one without the other. Therefore, plan for change, plan for the unexpected, and be strong when things do not go according to plan. Remember, change is a given; growth is a choice.

Keep rejection and refusal in proper perspective. As you discovered earlier in this book, people in sales hear "no" more often than any other professionals. You should build a wall to separate refusal from rejection. Refusal is professional and rejection is personal. When a prospect says "no" to your sales recommendation, you are on the professional side of the wall, and you shouldn't take it personally. As a professional, when you don't make a sale, you should study how to improve your professional skills. The refusal for your product or service was just that, a reason not to buy from you, the professional. Don't let a business decision made by a person whom you hardly know determine how you accept yourself. There are very few people who can reject you personally. These are usually the people who are closest to you. That is, your spouse, child, or other close relatives. If the prospect is not one of these people, he or she can't personally reject you! Learn to separate refusal from rejection.

If you can build on these foundation blocks, selling becomes easier—not easy, but easier. You can support a growing sales career by building on a solid foundation.

Now, go sell somebody something!

"I WANT A KNOWLEDGEABLE SALESPERSON!"

R ecently, one of my retail clients conducted a customer satisfaction survey. The number one response was, "I want a knowledgeable salesperson helping me." I asked how my client was interpreting that response. She said that she thought it meant that more training was needed in the area of product knowledge.

I suggested that she delve into the surveys a bit more. The reason for this suggestion is that most salespeople can learn product knowledge on their own by studying and/or using the products. They can read user's manuals. They can observe other salespeople assisting prospects. Most salespeople do not need more product knowledge.

What most salespeople do need is more knowledge of the prospect's needs, issue, and challenges. If the salesperson took the time to uncover the needs of the prospect, he or she would know what features of the product to demonstrate. He or she could then communicate the specific benefits of most value to the prospect.

As a case in point, a friend purchased her first cell phone. The young salesperson seemed expert in helping her. He showed her all the new phone's features and how to program it. He even knew what areas of town had the best reception and what areas were suspect. He had great knowledge about the phone and how it worked. The problem was that he had no knowledge of how my friend was going to use the phone, especially in the first weeks after purchasing it. She traveled to the East Coast several times for several days at a time. When she received her bill, the roaming charges were astronomical! (She later solved the billing problem, after lengthy phone calls and speaking to far too many customer service people.)

The point is this: had the salesperson taken the time to become "knowledgeable" about the buyer and her needs, she would not have had this problem. You add value as a sales professional when you have your "finger on the pulse" of the prospect, his needs and concerns, and his environment.

Now, go sell somebody something!

THE 3x5 CONCEPT FOR A BETTER HOME LIFE

H ere are three ideas for building a better life at home. Each of these ideas has five sentences. Thus, "The 3 x 5 Concept."

When should you tell your spouse you love him or her? The answer: before someone else does! Pretty obvious, isn't it? You need to tell your spouse you love him or her when he or she needs to hear it. Don't say it just when it is convenient for you! Be sensitive to the needs of your loved ones.

Make common courtesy a common practice. Common courtesy dictates that you call your spouse if you are going to be late coming home.

Common courtesy dictates that you listen to your children with all your senses. This includes your full attention: look them in the eye, with the television off and no newspaper or magazine in your hands. All of this is common courtesy. The challenge is to make it a common practice.

Your kids don't want quality time—they want you! Your spouse understands the concept of quality time; your children don't! They just want Mom and Dad. To kids, love is spelled T-I-M-E! You must spend time with your children; if you don't, they'll find someone who will!

Now, go sell somebody something!

WHAT DOES CRUISE CONTROL COST YOU?

I love the cruise control feature on my car. I can't imagine driving long distances without the use of cruise control. I mean, it's simple to use, it's safe, and there's no pressure. You just relax and put your feet back. You drive at a steady pace. You just take it easy. There is less mental fatigue. You just ease into it and the next thing you know, a couple of hours have passed. You can really get accustomed to using your cruise control. Sometimes you don't even know you have it engaged.

I remember the first car I owned with cruise control. At that time, the feature didn't come standard with the car and it cost about $350. Man, was it worth it!

Salespeople can engage a type of cruise control in their careers. And let me tell you, it ain't worth it! You slip your career into cruise control and you relax, put your feet back, and take it easy. There is less mental fatigue. And the next thing you know, a couple of hours have passed. Then a few days have passed; a couple of weeks have passed. Without your realizing it, an entire month has passed. You have eased into cruise control, and it's cost you a lot more than $350!

It's also costing you your professionalism, your pride, your reputation, your confidence; it could be costing you your career! You cannot afford the "cruise control" feature on your sales career. You drive your sales, you drive your earnings, and you drive your sales success. Fight the temptation to coast as a sales professional. Don't play it safe. Venture boldly into your sales activities each and every day. Set both short-term and long-term sales goals. Put an action plan together and "grow git 'em!"

Take your career out of cruise control. You'll be glad you did.

Now, go sell somebody something!

THE FIVE-STEP
SALES MEETING

Conducting a sales meeting can be a challenge. The following is an outline that offers a simple procedure for conducting an effective sales meeting.

Step 1: Begin with Motivation

Start the meeting with a short motivational message. This can be in the form of story and/or a recent sales victory. It can be taken from a sales book or self-help or motivational book or listening program. The manager can conduct this or can assign the segment to a salesperson. (The benefits of doing that are that it involves more people, it takes pressure off the sales manager, and it develops future leaders.) The time frame for this part is five minutes.

Step 2: Address Administrative Issues

Too often an entire sales meeting addresses administrative procedures and policies at the sacrifice of selling skills; therefore, this step should be fast, quick and to the point. Don't get trapped into elongating this step: its time frame is ten minutes.

Step 3: Goals and Goal Setting

Salespeople should be held accountable for setting and achieving sales objectives; therefore, each person should announce his or her goals for the coming sales period (i.e., week or month). The manager should have each person state his or her goals from the previous week and share with the group what goals were accomplished. This step's time frame is five minutes.

Step 4: Sales Skills Training

This is the most important step in the meeting. After all, it is the purpose of the "sales" meeting! The manager can address those issues that need the most improvement. The topics can include closing skills, managing objections, benefit selling, lead generation, etc. Again, the manager can assign this step to a salesperson. However, the manager must "inspect what you expect" by reviewing the presentation prior to the meeting. The time frame for this step is thirty minutes.

Step 5: Inspirational Close

The meeting should conclude on a high note—in an uplifting, positive manner. This can be accomplished by presenting awards, offering congratulations on previous sales victories, or sharing an inspirational story or message. The manager should conduct this step: the time frame is five minutes.

Now, go sell somebody something!

"First Touch the Person, Then Touch the Teeth"

D r. Richard Chapman has a very successful family dentistry practice in Plano, Texas. When asked the secret of his success, Dr. Chapman smiles (that's his way of advertising) and says, "My practice is built on a very simple concept. I teach my staff of professionals to first touch the person, then touch the teeth."

Dr. Chapman has built a successful practice because he addresses the people process before he addresses the dental process. In other words, he puts his patients first, ahead of their teeth. Oh, don't get me wrong. Dr. Chapman and his staff are very interested in teeth. They do a great job with the technical side of their practice. I have been a satisfied patient for more than nineteen years, as have the other members of my family. However, Dr. Chapman realizes that he is in the dental industry—but he is in the people business.

You are also in the people business. Much like Dr. Chapman, you also help in straightening and strengthening your "patients." You help people strengthen their careers, their families, and themselves. And in so doing, you put a smile on their faces!

Dr. Chapman knows that the old adage still applies: people don't care how much you know until they know how much you care—about them! Today in your selling efforts, communicate to your prospects and customers that they are important. Show them you care about them by putting their needs ahead of yours. By doing so, you'll touch a lot of people today.

Now, go sell somebody something!

SELL LIKE AN ACE AND YOU'LL BE TREATED LIKE A KING

I f you play your cards right, you can have a great sales day every day!

Let's take the ace from a deck of playing cards and form an acronym from it:

A = Attitude
C = Confidence
E = Enthusiasm

Attitude

What separates the successful, high-performing sales professionals from the "just on the verge of success" salespersons? It's not how they react to the positives in life . . . it's how they react to the negatives in life! It's the lemon/lemonade concept. Here's an example of maintaining the right attitude. Just after taking the oath as the fortieth president of the United States, Ronald Reagan was shot in an assassination attempt. While in the operating room, he said to the doctors, "I hope you are all Republicans!" Later in the day, he told his wife, "Honey, I forgot to duck!" Whether you liked President Reagan or not, I think you'll agree that's the type of attitude you can admire. That's the type of attitude you need to have each and every sales day.

Confidence

You must have confidence in yourself, in your abilities, in your company, and in your products and services. If you don't have confidence in those areas, how can prospects have confidence in you? They can't. Basketball great Larry Bird had confidence. Before the 1986 NBA All-Star Game, he competed in the three-point shooting contest, which he won. Prior to going onto the court to warm up, he turned to the other contestants and asked, "Hey, which of you guys is playing for second place today?" That's confidence.

Enthusiasm

Nothing great has ever been accomplished without enthusiasm! That doesn't mean you have to jump up and down, snort, shout, and flail your arms on a sales call. That's not enthusiasm—that's hysteria. Enthusiasm is that extra pep in your step, the pride in your stride. It also means getting excited internally about your family, your friends, your profession, your company, your abilities. And enthusiasm puts you into action. It's like when a young couple parked at the lake one night and the young woman said, "It would be great if you put the top down." Within three minutes, the young man had the car top down. Not bad, considering the car was not a convertible! That's enthusiasm!

Today, sell like an ACE. Maintain a positive ATTITUDE, build your CONFIDENCE, and show your ENTHUSIASM in all that you do. If you play your ACE, you'll be treated like a king!

Now, go sell somebody something!

HOW MUCH FASTER DO
YOU WANT TO BE?

S everal years ago, the coach of the Louisiana State
University track team, Boots Garland, conducted
a running clinic for some members of my daughter
Quinn's softball team. Coach Garland demonstrated
how to increase running skills and quickness. He
showed the players small details that would improve
their speed and their performance—things like hand
placement, arm movement, and foot positioning.
Some of the players were surprised that these techniques were so trivial, yet so critical.

Quinn was having a difficult time understanding
how these small running techniques were going to
help her become faster. So she asked, "Coach, do

you really think this will help improve my speed?"

Coach Garland hesitated for just a moment, then responded with a question of his own: "I don't know. How much faster do you want to be?"

Well, Quinn couldn't answer. She just wanted to be faster. But she didn't know how much faster. And she didn't know if these tiny changes in technique would lead to big results. However, she did understand that Coach Garland was asking her additional questions.

He asked her, "How much are you willing to give in order to get faster?"

"How willing are you to put forth the effort to improve your speed?"

"Do you really believe that you'll improve without getting involved in the improvement?"

These same questions can be asked of sales professionals.

"How much better do you want to be?"

"How much are you willing to give in order to increase your sales abilities?"

"Do you really believe that you can improve your selling skills without getting involved in that improvement?"

"What placement and positioning will allow you to be more successful?"

"What small sales activities can you perform that will produce big results?"

"Do these small activities include listening to sales CDs? Reading and re-reading sales books? Enrolling in a sales workshop?"

Obviously, those questions can only be answered by you. But, then again, how much better do you want to be?

Now, go sell somebody something!

You've Reached the End of the Book, But Not the End of Your Career!

Congratulations. You've made it all the way through this book. This accomplishment should be on your victory list.

I hope you enjoyed reading it as much as I enjoyed writing it. Even more, I hope you enjoy your journey through the world of professional selling as much as I have enjoyed mine.

Selling is a great way to make a living. Of all the helping professions, selling ranks among the best of them! Each day you have opportunities to help people become more successful, help make their lives easier, and add value to their personal, professional, and family lives. What a great way to make a living.

Congratulations also in developing yourself as a salesperson. Personal growth precedes professional growth! Therefore, you should invest more in yourself than you do in your career. My wish is that you continue to grow through your profession.

Let me encourage you to embrace the principles in this book, continue to believe in yourself as a professional, and enjoy this great profession of ours. Your greatest sales successes are ahead of you!

Now, go sell somebody something!

ABOUT THE AUTHOR

Bryan Flanagan is a salesman. He invested fourteen years with the IBM Corporation, learning the profession as a salesman, a "people manager" and a national sales instructor. From 1984 through 2004, Bryan served as Director of Corporate Training for Ziglar Training Systems in Dallas, Texas. Bryan founded Flanagan Training Group, Inc., and researches, develops, and delivers training programs in the areas of sales, sales management, and presentation skills. Bryan shares his educational, entertaining, and encouraging messages with more than 115 groups each year. He has fun, and so do his audiences.

Bryan lives with his wife Cyndi and their two children in Plano, Texas.

CONTACT THE AUTHOR:

Flanagan Training Group, Inc.
3912 Wilshire Drive
Plano, TX 75023
972-578-1820
www.flanagantraining.com
‹http://www.flanagantraining.com›
bryan@flanagantraining.com